LookBook:

Lauren Velasquez Robinson

BookLeaf Publishing

India | USA | UK

Presentation by *BookLeaf Publishing*

Web: www.bookleafpub.com

E-mail: info@bookleafpub.com

ISBN: 9789357695831

First edition 2023

DEDICATION

To Monique who helped me better understand myself, and made me feel emotions again. Thank you.

Tuesday: [Beep

Please leave a message for________________]

Hey ca..I guess you're busy..uhmm

[Press one to leave a message.]

-pressed 1-
Hi! So i was calling to see how you are? I'm fine, i was wondering if you have to-beat, beat, beat-your fist against your heart to show your heart how to keep beating? Cause I'm not sure..
[nervous laughter]

But don't worry, ya know, the -thump, thump, thump,- is actually pretty soothing, and I learned that, which you probably already know, people like patterns, like that's something we are always trying to figure out in life, soo this pattern-bum, bum, bum- has to be my pattern for life, right?

Anyways miss ya bestie, if you have time call me back!

It's Monday

and the stolen boxers fit
me so well, a cotton kindness
of a one-night-stand
the strands of fabric imprinted
with us quietly messing up
the sheets which i'll be too
tired to fix for days
too tired to change
too tired realize again
it's monday

Tuesday: I didn't know

How heavy my depression was;
until i got up from the shower floor and left a
depression
in the white tiles of my asscheeks

it sinks in me
this heaviness

and eventually i'll learn how long it takes
for the water to run cold: 53 minutes the length of
counting
the tiles and citing a prayer for each one

but I'll get up
with a hand from a ghost
wrapped in my brother's old-too-long-patchy-robe

to feel again;
or at least feel the velvetness of a cloth
15 years being worn down

Wednesday: Rose Colored Glasses

turned everything red
and our red flags looked
like celebratory flag markers
until the glasses broke

and i got blue contacts
and everything looked
like it was drowning in the middle of the desert
until they dried up

and now i just got my dry eyes
blinking continually clearing my vision
the colors so salty and dull;
a foothills thunderstorm baptism

Thursday: Haikus 1-4

My saint Flora of
Arvada, of forgiveness
of sadness, of fruit;

a twenty-nine year
damn broke, my whole soul weeping
for three straight days-

I wore borrowed clothes
to sit in a car crying
for only god knows what-

can i be a saint?
will God anoint me
Saint of Queer Failure?

Lavender **Monday** Hues

Something soft/ something poignant/ someone
sweetly humming
 hundred devotions to God, to my ancestors
in the purple hours of the morning
what's god's favorite flower to send to lovers?

 I ask her and kiss her sleeping eyes
 and put on wrinkled pants with my sunburnt
grandpa's hands
 place airpods from my lavender print case.
[cue sweet drums, a melody, cool rnb beat- "Wasn't
Looking"]

 Maybe she'll tell me later
 after my 8-hour shift at a shitty minimum-wage job
 across town in my mom's car

Friday:

god laughed in the places i've cried
and us, women, whose lips were sealed, cracked and
cried

cockscomb tears; collected in rain catchers by our
therapists
who tend to sugar cookie hearts, hoya hearts,

god relaxed in the places i've bounced my leg
uncontrollably
And i've carried my emotional cacti around to prick a
finger to feel tears, to cry

gold petals; swept up to decorate alters dedicated to
my lineage of comedian ghosts
joking around with god's angels whose stories left us
in warm tears;

god i found you in BlushnBlue's bathroom with
glitter makeup running down acne-scarred cheeks, i
showed her a little tenderness: our spilt lips kissed.

Saturday: Calm your anxiety

by making coffee for your
house guests
house ghosts
house ghouls

layout the moth-eaten tablecloth
hide it with bread and cookies
layout the brown-painted cups
chipped and mismatched

serve with sugar
serve with a warm milk
serve with a worry stone on each saucer

listen to the laughter
the woosh of coffee stirred
watch your anxiety pull up
and turn into the newest house guest

Tuesday

I'll grab a pair of black ripped jeans
from the floor, a black tank top,
and my "Dime Piece" screen printed wind-jacket.
drag myself into the costume;
the mirror an unfriendly companion suggests
A boy beat to hide
last night's nightmare glossed over eyes
bruised lips from anxious biting
and rosacea blooming like an oil painting

        -the newest edition to "Melancholy
Women"

Wednesday: LookBook

-Gold and camel's caramel hair accented jacket for luck
-Tortoiseshell, eggshells, pink salt grinded for protection
-Marigold and blood red cherries for ancestors
-Honeycomb, pomegranate seeds, and raw lips for spring offering
-Creamy milk and cinnamon on the first of the month prosperity
-Grapefruit, chocolate bruises and dark circles to be grounded
-Cayenne pepper, lavender nikes and graying strands for *return to sender*

Thursday: "Beginning Again

In life" i tried to google it to find some pretty advice or some quotes to recite/ nothing came up but questions for myself to answer/ what does it mean to begin again? How would I define that? wikihow did provide a 13 steps page with pictures "how to start over in life when you feel stuck"/ really i want an article about "how to start life when you thought it was over" or "you made it past what you thought you make it to, so now what"/ but here I am lost in my head, my heart is taking a 10, and i guess i am beginning again;

Friday: part 2

i'm beginning to cry strings of pearls which I then plant in a hanger above my head, and when they reach my pillow I'll trim them, cast them in purple plaster and loop a thrifted cross on it, and begin to recite my payers/ i'm beginning to bake again, and relearn the subtleties of love and patience in a permission cream tart, the act of healing through playing rnb music while dancing on cold floors while my ancestors sit on flour painted countertops clapping me on, i'll dance merengue with my tio frank's big yellow butterfly/ i'm beginning to fall in love in my mundane 6 step hair routine: brush, leave in conditioner, curly mousse, curly gel, curly spray, grab a small piece of hair and make a Evil-eye-catching braid and speak rosey-love and marigolds into it/ i'm beginning to take my emotions out for coffee on sunday and monday mornings to talk or draw how we are feeling, and I'll watch the generational-trauma-redline mini stats go down slowly, while sweet sadness hands me a tissue, a dead caterpillar, and a bottle of *real* vanilla/ i'm beginning the small irreversible acts of glory of dressing me in mixture of ruby reds and brothers pants, stolen hoodies and lavender fog jumpsuits, a swirling of emeralds and yellow bruises

Wednesday

I grab my late grandma's nail polish
Raisin-The-Bar
a 1970s sweet pink metallic look
remodeled with nostalgia old hollywood
a nail bottle of "*kiss-me-boss*"
and "*my daddy taught me to throw a punch*".

Here i sit in zoom with camera off
in class painting my nails instead.
Humming to music, double-checking
the teacher can't hear or see me
transforming my slightly indented nails
into a calming power.
Each stroke flashes a moment
from my grandma's life-
       her running,
       kitchen stories,
       babies crying,
       her crying
       on porch steps brushing my hair
       passing on food,
       gifting me her blues-
I seal the polish with a topcoat
sealing her fate onto my nails
working women
educated women
taking care of the home women
alone women
Raising-the-bar, but at what cost

Thursday

Her reddened eyes
her face seeks consolation from her hand
her pose of surrender legitimizes her letting go

her perfume bottle on its side
knocked over,
arousing the surrounding patrons

the exposed crease between the arm and armpit
the flannel jacket a shawl
screams quietly, "look, I don't care"

delicate thrifted drapery
in an abyss of mascara tears
offers up her charm and fullness to onlookers

Friday

Grab your Staple Pieces for Sadness
right when you wake up
and the blue shades tint the afternoon light
and the robin cream-speckled sheets
drape around you like cigarette smoke.

wear the checkered bolo-tie
and green rain slip dress
with the black boots, tights, and white Star Wars socks
secure the wooden-jaguar earrings
and put on the aspen embroidered jean shirt you sewed
with a second layer of green north face jacket, for puff.

A yellow silk scarf with red roses to protect your energy
lavender-filled pockets for luck
sage stuffed socks to attract goodness
and fill your purse with tobacco as a peace offering

And step back out into the world

Monday: Gloria Tells Me

To get up and get dressed/ she rolls up the curtain and sweeps away the dead flies and mumbles a curse/ she lights a white candle and chuckles with the house ghost/ she sits me on the wicker bench and combs out the knots in my curls/ she fixes my waves to mimic the rolling hills outside, adorned with pops of silver pearls and tells me laughingly "Imma strong one"/ her fingers wrapping around each 2c strand like a prayer she's setting into motion/ i ask "why haven't I had an emotional release yet?"/ she grabs some green clips to set some waves on my face and stays silent

Tuesday: part 2

Gloria sits in front of me and puts her head in my lap and tells me about a decision she met at the grocery store off at N. Pecos st./ she tells me the coffee packages sit around together after hours gossiping, Ms. Buestole with Mr. Pilon and Abuelita sharing sauce recipes and bragging about their grandchildren whose throats sew the new lands with red chile and tobacco are doing fine/ she tells me the butcher is a reluctant messiah who stuffs little fortunes and parables into the fresh meat and fish sometimes, but my grandma flora would mistake it for fat and throw it away, but the dog would eat it and be immediately granted into doggie heaven/ she tells me to thump the fruit, play them all like musical instruments and instructs me how to play each one; shake the dragon fruit, grab a stick to run across a guanabana, click-clack the bananas, castanent the pomegranates, and of course flute the papaya/ she tells me love lingers in the spice section, and to never grab more than 3 spices at a time otherwise love will follow you around the store and hop in your plastic bag and when you get home it becomes sour and attaches itself to the next pretty woman who comes over/ she tells me that she decided that it's better to grocery shop blindfolded, it's easier to figure it out at home; to cook the different flavors of emotions and feed them to your kids, friends and neighbors, but she couldn't mix the right ones together to feed me/ gloria tells me she can't teach me to grocery shop or cook because it's been tainted bitter but that's the way she likes it, and decided with the checkout girl i'll learn alone and they hand me my own shoppers card

Saturday

I dropped off my pink baggage
at the airport, loaded at terminal C
got back into my car, drove home
saluted the blue horse
and blew a kiss at myself in the rearview mirror
admired my manicured metallic hands on the
steering wheel.
Adorned with grandma's rings
and my grandpa's flannel shirt hugging me
my iron black pants, and cleaned boots holding me
my brother's old Faried shirt nodding with me
it's peace in a car ride
it's sweetness in an outfit

Wednesday: It's Looking Up

I caught her eye from the passenger side. Walking with a slight hop in my black sambas, black jumpsuit with brown hoodie-the music was just right, the weather was crisp, sunny, my tio's butterfly walked with me.

 "YOU ARE pretty cute! I like youurr style! Hey!" with an infectious passed-down smile from happy woman

 she yelled while rolling down her window on the silver and white two-door Honda. A cigarette licking her middle and forefinger, ashes falling on her rose-tattooed hand. Her hair waving by like prairie grass, as the car kept driving

 her ancestors piled in a car behind her, a support team, a parade promoting kindness

Sunday

i wore my sunday best
according to you

-burnt orange faux leather pants
-sunflower yellow hoodie with print reading "pray"
"pray" "pray"
-a white mask with painted tears
-a memorizing blue fisherman hat

drop the match
the flame following the gas
i'm all lighted up for you

sincerely,
the villain

Monday: What is the "Boy Beat"? Black Out Poem

Sir J
revealed his makeup vision for some most
unforgettable   eyes

 a shape, giving the cheeks a shape
 You see how much chiseling is happening here?
That's on purpose.
 capture her essence give her structure give her power

 "The Boy Beat" where she
          accentuating features that we usually
would consider flaws, like rosacea, acne, dark circles,
tears, feeling low difficult to define
          unique ways.

 My own personal 'boy beat', for example, is when I
neglect plucking my monobrow for a few weeks, [or
when I open up a pallet of emotions to friends]

[It's] an androgynous way to look at makeup [at
depression] being masculine and feminine at the
same time, adding a bit more structure, [a bit more
visibility]
 It's certainly not a new phenomenon
 but it's worth unpacking.

she writes: "It's very refreshing to take a break from using winged liner, overdrawn lips [and] exaggerated cat eyes just to achieve the goal of looking hyper-feminine [instead i can just cry, allow my tired eyes to be my eyeshadow, to show my femininity]."

Instead, we're met with fresh skin, brushed-up brows, and balmed lips [and full blue emotions on display]
Then there's the pièce de résistance – the dark circles. Come again?
accentuate their exhaustion
My regular sad face, skin complexion, but make it fashion." just accepting them
let us always embrace the frecks [the flaws, the sadness]
to look beat or beat up.
Why not? "It has nothing to do with your flaws as much as it has to do with a modern approach to Being vulnerable, to talking about depression. It's more about an unintentional effortless approach to beauty to being yourself.
the look is about "[loving] yourself and the skin you're in [and experiencing it all]."